GREATER THAN ONE

BRANDON A. VOCI

Dedicated to all the people who work to make this country a wonderful place.

———————————————————————————

To those who may feel their voices are not heard.

AUTHOR'S NOTE

About one year ago, I decided to write my message of hope for the uncertain future that loomed over our beautiful nation. I firmly believe that everyone has the power to make this country a better place. Now, one year later, I remain a firsthand witness of an increasing amount of civil unrest that tears the moral fabric of our country apart. This conflict stems from a number of problems that we have come to face on a daily basis. Whether it is deep seated racial divisions, fear of different religions and cultures, or fear of change, it is essential that we all work to take a step in the direction of peace.

1

My generation has seen an increase in poverty and
mistrust in our own neighbors. During my lifetime, I dream of a
world that is more peaceful and prosperous for all. We must find
a way to end this unrest and mistrust; only then can
we achieve our goals as a nation.

   All of us who call this country home must work to unite. All of
us must conquer our fears. All of us must work to create a better
future. We are a nation that is greater than one. Greater than one
race. Greater than one religion, and greater than one idea.

–BRANDON A. VOCI

2

This is the United States of America.

It is the land of **OPPORTUNITY.**

3

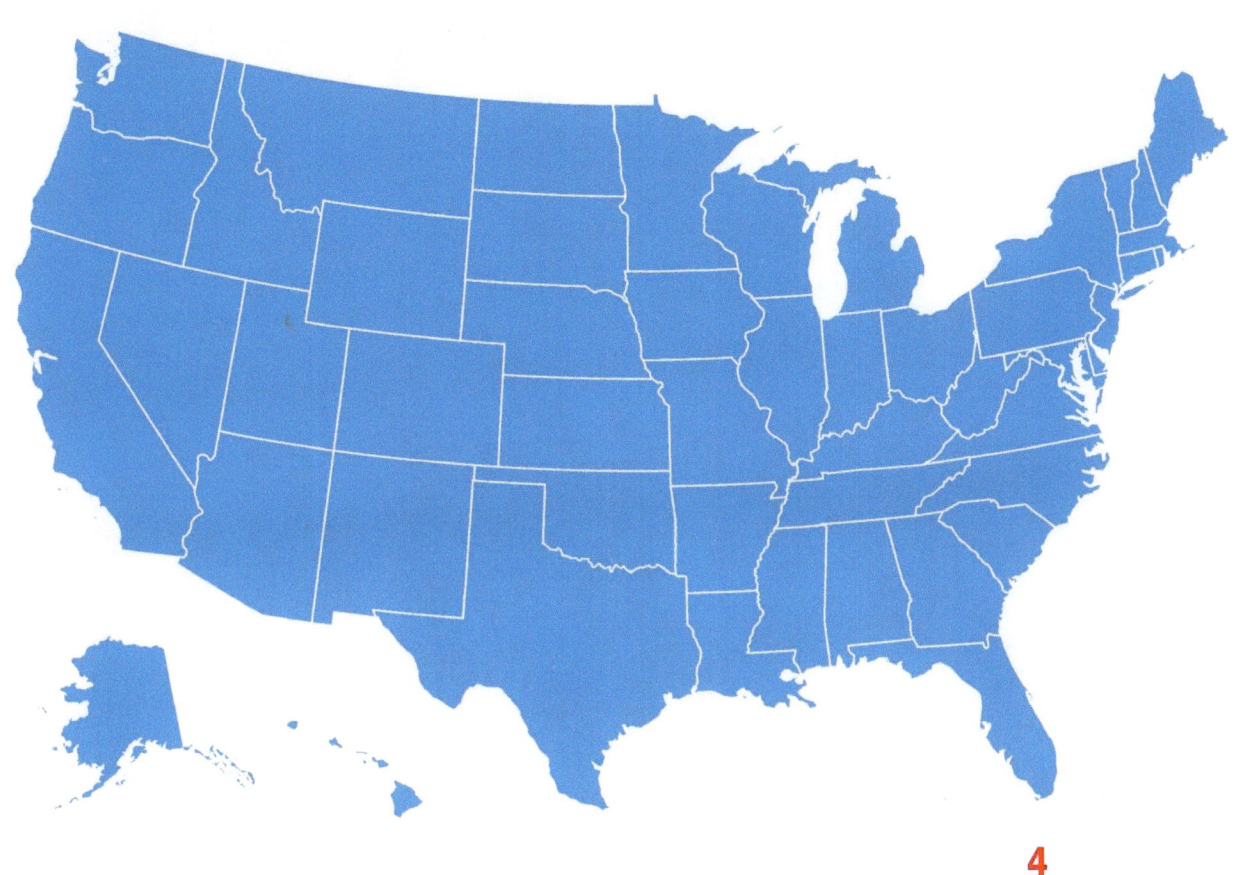

4

WE look different,

WE have different religions,

but we are all united by our love for this country, the United States of America.

5

We may have roots in every continent, but we all proudly call ourselves AMERICANS.

7

8

The reasons our ancestors came here were very clear. They wanted to be part of something better and new. A place where everyone could be RESPECTED and VALUED.

9

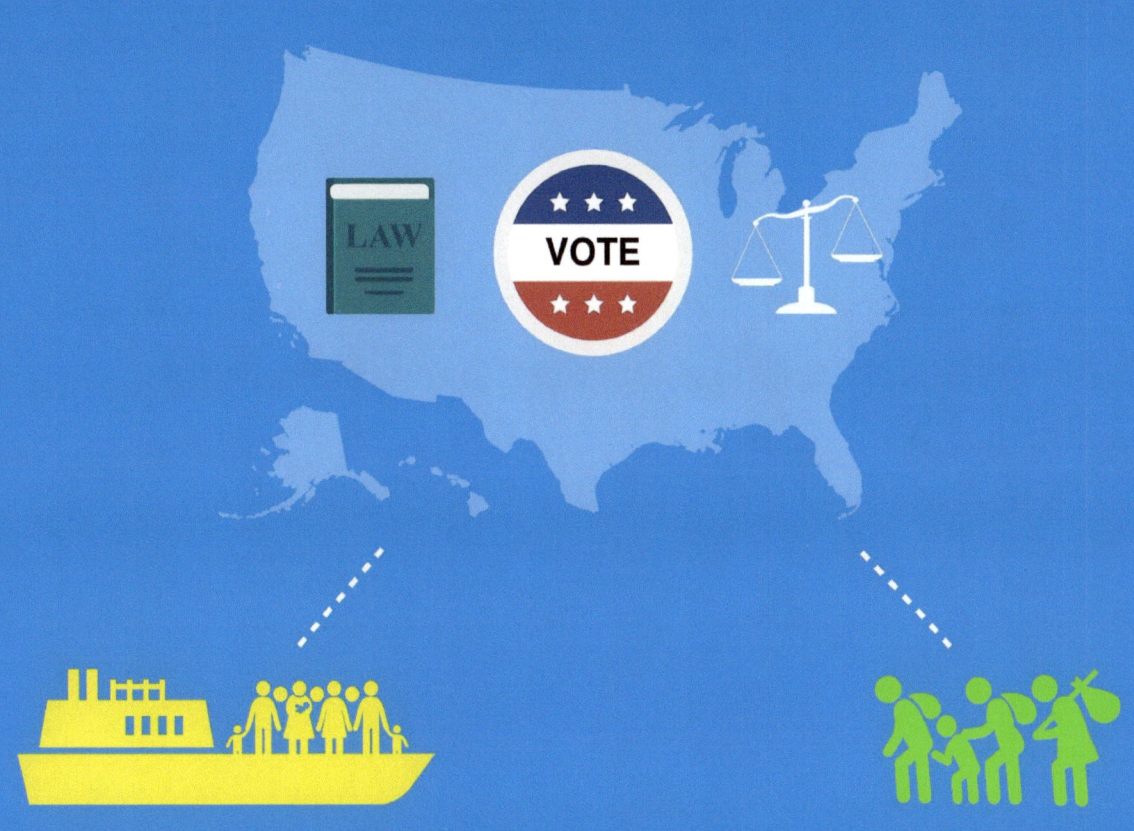

We are all united by common **GOALS** and **BELIEFS**, helping us through times of hardship and connecting us together.

11

12

We must work together as **ONE**.

Together we can look towards our future without fear.

UNITED, we will achieve our dreams of a future that is prosperous and fair for everyone.

13

We must work with our neighbors to create a more **PEACEFUL, SAFE** and **JUST** community.

15

The task lies on all of our shoulders, no matter how young or old. We all have something to contribute.

17

18

The future belongs to all of us. We all have the **POWER** to shape it and make it how we want it to be.

19

Each and every one of us has something to give; something meaningful to contribute.

LET'S LISTEN TO ONE ANOTHER!

21

WE ARE GREATHER THAN ONE!

23

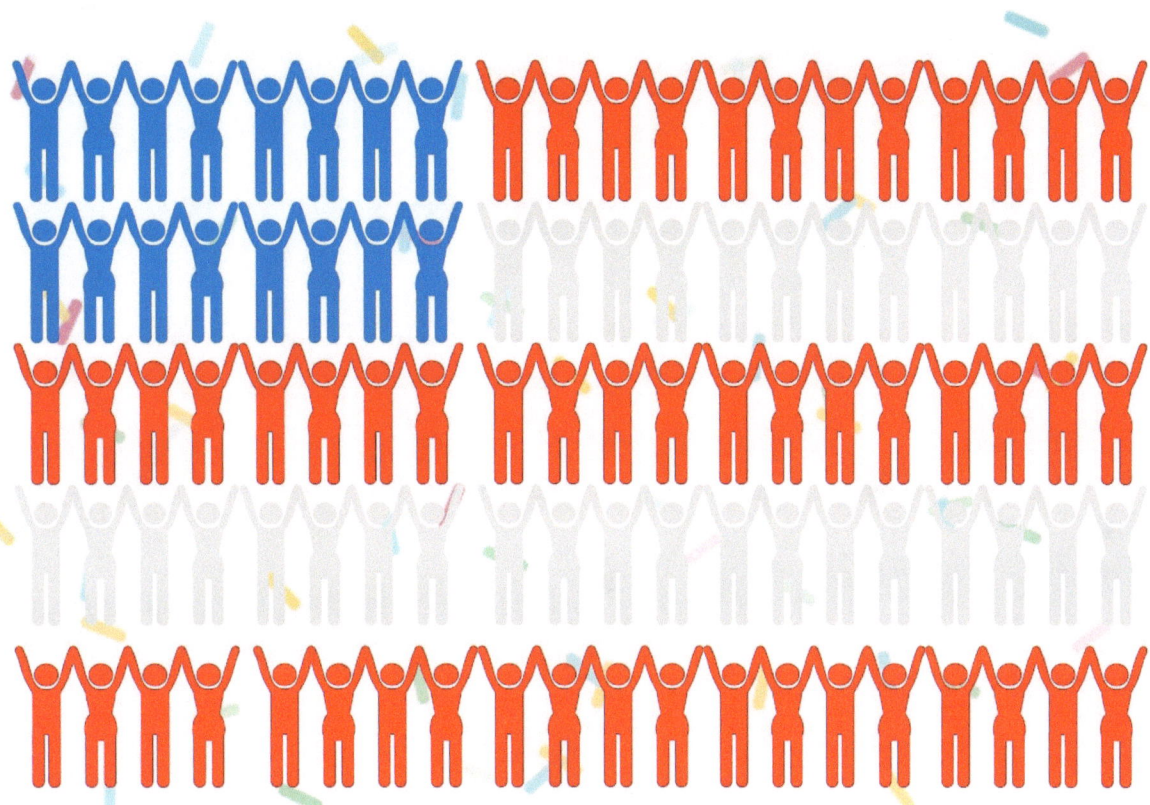

24

ACKNOWLEDGMENTS

The support of my whole family has been inspiring. I am so lucky to have you all in my life.

Special thanks to all the exceptional teachers I have met along the way. So many of them continue to inspire me to write and advocate for what I believe in.

Lastly, I would like to commend all of the people that still believe in this country. The people who still believe in equality and justice for all. We must continue to fight for this idea.

25

ABOUT THE AUTHOR:

Brandon Voci is a 10th grade student at Wellesley High School, in Wellesley

Massachusetts. Genuinely concerned with the future welfare of our beautiful nation,

Brandon published the "Faces of America" at age 13. In it, he reminded readers that we are

a nation built by immigrants and therefore we should celebrate our rich diversity.